He's Just

NOT

Dating Deal Breakers

Kim
"Have You Lost Your Mind?"
Samuels

He's Just NOT: Dating Deal Breakers

Published by Wheatmark®
610 East Delano Street, Suite 104
Tucson, Arizona 85705 U.S.A.
www.wheatmark.com

ISBN: 978-1-58736-735-9
LCCN: 2006937838

This book is dedicated to Dawn.
Your life was not in vain ...

Acknowledgments

I am lucky to have great friends to be able to thank. They are always there to listen to tales of my escapades and to be supportive, even on the rare occasion when I am exasperated. We have been through many of the "Oh, hell no!" and "You are making that up!" moments. Needless to say, we've had untold hours of unbridled laughter.

Thanks to my cheerleaders: Michelle, Renee, Mae, Lisa, Marilynn, Emma, Sharronn, Dorotea, La Tonya, Kimberly, and Kris. For my male support system, thanks to Ronnie, Keith, and Jeffrey. Thanks also to Risa and Holly for your invaluable input.

Contents

Introduction

Women need to realize sooner when a man is just not that into them. There are many, many signs that men give us along the way. We can choose to ignore them or believe friends who tell us that we're just being too judgmental. It's easy to be dismissive or, worse yet, to refuse to believe even the most obvious telltale signs, all in the name of having a man. Why? Are we *that* desperate? We need to stop making excuses for men and open our eyes wide from the first second of contact. Be aware when people show you who they are and believe them. Actions really do speak louder than words, but words can speak volumes, too. I pay attention to both actions and words. After all, as the saying goes, "Fool me once, shame on you. Fool me twice, shame on me." If I let someone fool me three times, just smack me.

My friends think I am too picky at times. I don't call it being picky; I call it not accepting anything I don't like or anything that raises the slightest flag. In other words, I don't take any shit.

I told this to a guy one time, and he asked me what that meant. I said, "If I am not treated how I feel I should be treated, it is immediately over."

He sarcastically asked, "Oh, does that mean you want to be treated like a queen?"

I, just as sarcastically, replied, "How about just being treated like a human being?" If a guy can't treat me with everyday respect, what the fuck do I want him for? If a guy starts out in the negative, why should he get a second chance at anything?

I took a break from dating. It was a self-imposed "I don't feel like being bothered for a while" break that lasted about a year and a half. Then, after re-entering the dating field, I tried Internet dating for over a year. Why does dating take so much energy? I can tell you why. It's because ninety-five percent of the men are lying. Yes, I said it. Don't even try to tell me I'm exaggerating, either, because I have my own personal stats to prove it.

I identified a few deal breakers by just sitting down, doing some introspection, and deciding what I absolutely didn't want in a mate or a dating partner.

Deal Breaker #1: Has Little Kids

How little is a "little kid" to me? I'd say anything under fifteen years old. Why? Because my son is twenty-six years old and I feel like I am now on parole having served my time. Like it or not, raising a child is just like doing time. You do at least eighteen years to life. I am also rehabilitated and have no desire to do another stint. Plus, my patience is long gone. A couple of years ago, I tried to date a guy with a small child, and I had to be honest with myself: I wanted to kill the little mothafucka! Just keepin' it real, people, just keepin' it real. By the way, I curse, and, yes, I mentioned it in my online dating profile.

I have corresponded with quite a few guys who felt that I did not give them a fair chance. After all, they reasoned, they might be my soul mate, and I wouldn't talk to them, all because they had small children. But why would I want to start something—anything—with them if I did not want to interact with their children? I cannot fathom why a guy would want to be bothered with me if I didn't want to be bothered with his children. Trust me, if he were my soul mate, God would have made sure he did not have little kids.

Deal Breaker #2: Lives with His Mother

If he lives with his mother, and is not there for caretaking purposes, this means he can't or won't take care of himself. I am not taking care of anybody anymore. I have seen that side of the road, and I have no desire to cross the street. I know there are some women out there who will gladly take care of a man, even way past the "he's just not that into you" stage. I, however, am not one of them.

Deal Breaker #3: Has Been to Prison

Past, present, and future parolees need not apply. Why, you ask? That's just me, one of my preferences. If he's turned his life around, then I'm very happy for him. However, that does not mean I want him as my mate. I get a lot of flack on this, even from women. I can't understand why people so desperately want me to date ex-cons or why they think I'm being totally unreasonable. They say, "Everyone makes mistakes, and you can't hold it against them forever." Yeah well, I'm not holding shit against anyone, and life's not fair. Get over it.

One of my deal breakers may not be one of yours and vice versa. Don't let other people try to talk you out of your deal breakers. Repeat them. Memorize them. Embrace them. Most of all, don't let the penis cloud your senses. Step away from the penis until you have eliminated your deal breakers.

Sure, there might be times when you really don't care because you're just horny. But that doesn't mean that when you return from la-la land, he should be a serious prospective mate. Do not confuse *She's Gotta Have It* with *From Here to Eternity*. Don't get it twisted, yo. (That's Ebonics for "keep it straight in your head.") Again, always listen to what people say to you. I may keep repeating this to make sure you do indeed listen. File things away if you're not sure. This means to not be dismissive of signs and to make a mental note of them for future reference.

My whole intention in even trying Internet dating was to meet a nice guy, possibly have a monogamous relationship with him, and see where it could go from there. Forever optimistic, I never would have believed how hard that would be. I had no idea of the eventual outcomes or what valuable lessons I would learn. The main lesson I learned was how hard it was to meet someone who doesn't make you want to punch him in the face. Why? There are many, many various reasons that you are getting ready to find out about.

The idea to write this book came about after one particularly crazy-ass dating episode. I was sitting at my kitchen table, reflecting, when my spirit told me to write a book. I did not set out looking for material. Whether that appeases those who I've dated or not, I really don't care. I am a comedian, so sometimes I would jot down notes about some funny things that happened. I thought that I might be able to use some of the stuff in a sitcom that I had developed and was writing for cable. Unfortunately or fortunately, depending on how you look at it, I couldn't find a way to use those anecdotes for that project, so they were just in a pile of notes. Life keeps showing me that you never know when stuff will come in handy.

Names have been removed to protect the guilty.

Gold Teeth and More

This was one of my very first Internet dates. OK, so I had talked to this guy quite a few times, and he was a hoot. He had a great sense of humor, a great laugh, and a sexy southern accent. He had me howling with laughter on the phone. He said things like, "Once you meet me, baby, you're never gonna want to leave me." He asked me, "You gonna make me your love slave, sunshine?" A person who says things like that definitely has to have the right stuff to back it up. He told me he was fifty, but he sounded young at heart. We decided to meet for lunch. In his picture, he was wearing a uniform of some sort, he was not smiling, and he had a trim build.

I got to the restaurant first, put my name down on the seating list, and called him to see what his estimated time of arrival was. He was about eight minutes away, and I stayed on the phone for a couple of minutes, giving him further directions. When he was almost there, the table was ready, so

I sat down and ordered beverages. When I finished ordering, I went back to the reception desk to meet him and take him to our table.

I heard this guy say, "Oh, there she is." Luckily, if you can call it that, he recognized me, since I looked like my picture. I would never in a million years have recognized him from his picture. The picture must have been twenty years old, and he did not look fifty—he looked sixty years old. If I remember correctly, his height was listed on his profile as five-feet ten-inches. Now, I am five feet five inches. I was wearing one-inch heels, and he was not taller than me. In what lifetime was he five-feet ten-inches? He was wearing a long, sleeveless exercise shirt with matching pants. The pants had the added benefit of noisily announcing the fact that he was walking because his thighs rubbed together (swish, swish, swish, swish as he moved). I swear I am not making this shit up. He had a huge stomach—so much for an athletic build—and straightened hair. Just then, yes, he opened his mouth and showed me his gold "fronts." This means his front teeth had gold on them. Inwardly, I was screaming like the kid in the movie *Home Alone* when he smacks the aftershave lotion on his face. Outwardly, I turned around and made the "child looking at food like it's nasty" face. It's right up there with the ugly cry face—not cute. I walked in front of him to the table and watched the crazy, wild stares of the other patrons. I felt like I was having an out-of-body experience. What in the world were the other customers thinking? He looked like an old-school pimp. I, then, must have looked like one of his "working girls." *Great, now I'm a ho.*

He looked nothing like his picture. I had the urge to show

him his profile, tell him to look in a mirror, and ask him if in any way, shape, or form he resembled his picture. Why didn't I run? I just don't know how to explain it. I was riveted. I acted like everything was hunky-dory, went ahead and ate lunch, and chatted. Later, my girlfriend asked me why I didn't bolt. My only explanation was that I was like a deer in headlights: frozen. I kept trying to avert my gaze from the gold teeth. I tried to remain even-keeled. I kept the conversation going in a varied and detached way. I even ignored the fact that he dropped food on his protruding "athletic" stomach, which left an indelible tomato sauce stain.

At that moment I knew, deep down, that I could act. This was my first leading role. I was so good, even I couldn't believe it. We finished lunch, which seemed like it lasted three freakin' years, and then he walked me to my car. God knows how I restrained myself from literally running to the damn car. I could feel the stares from people, but I refused to make eye contact with anyone. I might lose it, break out of character, and die laughing. I casually said, "I'll be in touch," knowing that was an out and out lie. I just wanted to get away without any public drama. Once inside my car I breathed a deep sigh of relief. That was extra special. Sing to the melody of *The Twilight Zone* theme song: Do do do do, do do do do. Why me? That had to be retribution for something I had done in my life. Whatever it was, that debt was definitely paid in full.

I wanted an alcoholic beverage real bad. I rushed home, poured some wine, and called my friend Renee while I amended my online profile. I added, "Do not respond if you have gold teeth or if your picture is twenty years old." I recounted the whole date to Renee, and I was damn near tears with laughter. I asked her, "Did I mention he had a shag?" I almost peed on myself. How could I have forgotten that?

It was after this date that I decided that a first meeting should just be something very simple and quick. Starbucks would soon become a major part of my life, and I don't even drink coffee. Ladies, if you are looking for a free meal, let it go. Trust me when I tell you it is not worth it.

Delete gold teeth's telephone number. Next ...

More Than Twenty Minutes Late

This guy was pleasant enough on the phone and was a pretty good conversationalist. One thing I remember, though, was that he kept asking me if I'd ever been skydiving or jet skiing and other things that were somewhat expensive. He implied that he would be taking me, which, of course, was a ruse. He just threw that in to make me think he had money. I was not fooled; I just filed it. This is a big thing for me, mentally filing stuff. I listen. I may not react to some things in the moment, but I will file information away for future reference. These little details can give you some insight into the real person. Bottom line: he was a bullshit artist.

We set a date to meet at noon at a restaurant—not for lunch, though. Initially, we wanted to see how the chemistry went. I was there at ten to noon. At ten after noon, I called a girlfriend and asked her how long I should wait before I left. She said twenty minutes. I was thinking fifteen minutes, but I said OK, I'd throw in five minutes.

He called me right after I hung up with my girlfriend and told me he had an emergency meeting and would be there in fifteen minutes. That would make him twenty-five to thirty minutes late.

I said, "OK, no problem," and left. I don't wait well. Plus, I felt that if he knew he was already going to be late he should have called me before he was late. Fuck him. In my older age, I am less accepting of stupid shit. Good-bye, and good riddance I said to myself as I left the restaurant. I never called him again. I guess he got the point.

Delete Mr. Can't Tell Time's telephone number. Next ...

The Bottomless Pit

I really liked this guy's voice on the phone. He was originally from the East Coast, so he got my sense of humor, and we seemed to be compatible. We set up plans to meet at Starbucks.

He looked better than his picture and had these gorgeous green eyes. He was a little heavier than I preferred, but I tried not to judge too quickly. *Give him a chance*, I told myself.

We talked for a while and decided to go five minutes away to a sports bar for a snack. Well, one person's snack is ... He ate—I mean, inhaled—twenty-four buffalo wings at record speed. All of those bones were squeaky clean. I just sat there and watched in awe. He offered me one, but I was scared to take it; I might have pulled back part of a finger. Next, he ordered this huge ice cream and cookie dessert, which he quickly wolfed down. *A little hungry, are we?* I thought in amazement.

I was shocked by this man's behavior, especially at a first

meeting. This is when someone should put his or her best foot forward. Unbeknownst to me at the time, I was slowly being introduced to a series of lessons: When people show you who they are, believe them. As women, we need to be keenly aware of everything that people show us from the very beginning. I did not feel that I needed to see any more from this man. After all, he wasn't as into me as he was his food. I suddenly became able to predict the future; in it, he was humongous. I couldn't help thinking, *Here comes the Pillsbury Dough Boy.*

Delete Humongo's telephone number. Next …

The Alcoholic

This was yet another one who gave good phone. He played the "really interested in me" game. We could stay on the phone for an hour at a time. Eventually, he confessed to the fact that, in addition to his two grown children, he had an eight-year-old. Now, if you remember, deal breaker #1 was no little kids. Maybe it's me, but an eight-year-old sounds little. Also, on his profile he only listed two children, so that was the first lie. In a subsequent conversation, I extracted from him that he did not drink. Next, he told me he didn't handle liquor well. Finally, he told me he was an alcoholic. All of this was told to me in stages. I revealed to him that my ex-husband was an alcoholic and that that was what ended our marriage. He sympathized with me but tried to assure me that this wouldn't present a problem with us. Yeah, right.

The night before we were to meet, I was stressed out. I was at a concert with a girlfriend. We were having a great time, just having some drinks and enjoying the show. My mind kept going back to this guy. What would it be like to date him? If we were out, I would not be able to have a drink in deference to him. I would have to put my enjoyment of a glass of wine on the back burner out of respect for his problem. Been there, done that.

Also, I just had a gnawing feeling that something wasn't right. I wasn't sure entirely what "it" was, but I have learned that I don't have to figure out what "it" is. All I need to know is that when something does not feel quite right, I should trust my instincts. Yes, I was a scaredy-cat and called him really late at night. I left a message that I was canceling the meet and greet. I felt a weight lifted off my shoulders and knew immediately it was the right decision. He called me the next day after his AA meeting (stop laughing) to try to talk me into still meeting him. I would not capitulate. His reasoning was that we were soul mates (oh, please), that we were destined to meet (of course), and that I should not let a little thing like his alcoholism stand in the way. Hmmm. A little thing like his alcoholism? What? What planet was he on? Not such a little thing. Then, he wanted to turn the tables on me. Well, how much did I drink since I didn't think I could be around him and not drink. It had nothing to do with how much I drank but with the fact that I indeed did so at my leisure and was not willing to change myself for someone I had not even met! Shit, I had a hard enough time with my ex, and I had known him since I was five fucking years old. *Bye-bye—go away.* I'll tell you what ... after dealing with him, I wanted a drink.

Delete lying alcoholic's telephone number. Next ...

White Zinfandel and Track Lighting

Do you remember the movie *Steel Magnolias?* The ladies were in the beauty shop and they were talking about how if a guy was into track lighting, he was gay? Keep this bit of information in the back of your mind. File it.

This guy sent me a really sweet note that said I looked like a goddess, what every woman wants to hear, and he asked how he could ever be fortunate enough to meet me. He asked me to not judge his picture too harshly; it looked like a mug shot, and said that his friends already told him to change it because he looked so much better than his picture. During that initial phone conversation, he told me to hold on a second. When he came back to the phone, he explained that he was in the middle of installing track lighting. "Warning, Will Robinson, warning." (This is for my older friends who remember the television show *Lost in Space.*) I told him to call me back when he was done. I could not get that conversation from *Steel Magnolias* out of my head. When he finally called me back, we continued talking about inconsequential things to get to know each other better. It turns out he drank white zinfandel.

I remembered an old email I got a long time ago that broke down different types of people by what they drink. It said that if men drank white zinfandel, they were gay. So, I deduced that track lighting and white zinfandel together scream "gay." You might come to his defense and say, "But he was talking to you." Yeah, well, you can also add the possibility of his being on the "down low" or add being bisexual to the equation. Either way, I didn't care to find out.

Bye-bye. I didn't even need to delete the number since I didn't have a chance to enter it.

Physical Deformities and Health Issues

This is a very touchy subject. Does it just scream shallow? No. I am in no way saying that the perfect man has to be perfect. What I am saying, though, is that certain things should be discussed, or at least disclosed, from the beginning. Not doing so is what I call deception and misrepresentation. Pictures online can be very favorable to some people. They will not show a clubfoot; yes, I met him. They may mask with sunglasses really bugged or crossed eyes; yes, I met both of them, too. Pictures don't show severe diabetes or prostate problems. Yes, I also had the unfortunate experience of a possible prostate problem.

If you are in a wheelchair, you must give advance warning of this prior to meeting a potential partner. This is not how you should "roll up" on someone. (Pun intended.)

A girlfriend told me that you should also let her know if

you are shorter than five feet five inches and are missing one leg—just a suggestion to you men.

More suggestions from some friends: Don't declare possessing a large member when it is actually three inches or less and bent. Staying on this same subject, please let a mothafucka know if you've got twelve inches with a diameter of three inches. Was he a horse in a former life? Not everyone can handle all of that.

My poll on this subject showed that some of these things did not necessarily turn women off, but, rather, the nondisclosure prior to their meeting did.

Athletic Build

There were so many guys that listed their build as athletic. It was amazing. My, oh, my. And they say women are the ones with body-type issues. At least we usually say we are bigger than we think we are and not the other way around.

The guy from The Gold Teeth and More chapter appeared to be twelve months pregnant when I met him. Then there was one guy who said that his picture was four years old but that he still looked the same. No, he didn't! His stomach was flat in the picture, and he showed up looking eight months pregnant. Not the same. "Looks the same" does not refer only to the face. Plus, you guys might think you still look the same in the face; however, you need to come on back to reality.

One guy was close to athletic, since he was only six months pregnant. He called himself athletic because his arms were somewhat muscular. Go figure.

Putting on athletic wear, a.k.a. workout clothes, does not

transform a body into an athletic body. Guys, just because you wear sneakers, it does not mean you have exercised—you've got to *move*. In case you do not know what different body-type descriptions really mean, let me break it down for you (and most guys round down, meaning if they say average, they've probably got more than a few extra pounds):

Body Types	Definitions
Slender	Skinny
Athletic	Nice to great build
Average	Could use some sit-ups for a paunch
A few extra pounds	Overweight; couch potato
Big and beautiful	Huge; obese

Guys, let me give you the two scenarios that scream "your build is not athletic":

A) Dunlap: "Your stomach Dunlap over your thighs."

B) Dicky-Doo: "Your stomach sticks out further than your dicky-doo." I ended up putting this one on my profile, because I got so tired of guys showing up with their pregnant stomachs.

A male friend of mine told me I was wrong for being particular about a guy's build. Excuse me? Men get away with this shit day in and day out. They even get very detailed with many female body parts and what size they should or should not be in order to be attracted to them.

OK, truth be told, I didn't actually voice the other preference, which was the size of the "dicky," because how do you say that without being crude or rude? Fine. Fuck it. You

27

best be packin', too. I like surprises but only if they're big. Don't try to be cute either and say you got six when you've measured it in centimeters. I may start carrying a ruler. I'm joking.

Size is the one thing we have little or no chance of figuring out from pictures or meeting for a latte. I've tried to come up with a possible line to say to a guy so that I can get a heads-up, if you will, as to the size. It's something along the lines of "If I were to buy condoms for you, what size would I get" too obvious? Does that line from the movie *Field of Dreams* apply to condoms: "If you build it, they will come"? If you buy large condoms large penises will come? I'll go with wishful thinking on that one.

A girlfriend of mine told me a story about this guy she slept with. She was waiting and waiting and thought that maybe it was his finger that she was feeling. She said she wanted to yell, "Come on, stop playin'. Seriously, stop playin'. Move your finger! Stop playin'." OK, that's not a cute predicament to be in. Where do you go from there? Certainly not up. That's funny. I crack myself up.

Threatens to Cut My Hair

A tall drink of water. That's how I referred to him when I saw his picture. We hit it off immediately over the phone. From the start, I told my friends he was like the male version of me. He spoke his mind and at times could be brutally honest. He kept me laughing. He also said what other people might think but would never actually say out loud. My friends say I do the same thing, which is true.

Our first meeting was at a Starbucks. We talked easily, and one of the employees there knew him. She stopped and talked with him for a while and told me, "I love this guy. He says whatever is on his mind." Her comment instantly made me feel more comfortable. It was, at the very least, confirmation that he was known and liked by someone.

We dated for about a month, and during that time he kept pulling my tail (long hair at the nape of my neck). He repeatedly told me that it was way out of style and that one day he was going to get a pair of scissors and cut it off. Excuse you?

What yo' problem is? My hair didn't bother him enough to prevent him from sleeping with me. *I put that nicely, didn't I?* I looked him in the eye and very seriously told him that would be the end of us. He laughed. I didn't. I wanted to make sure I was clear so I pointedly said, "I am serious." He told me he was just as serious about cutting my hair.

My hair makes a statement. It's my trademark and goes right along with my stand-up comedy stage name, "Have You Lost Your Mind?" It says, screams actually, "I don't give a fuck what anyone thinks!" I think that is quite obvious. Anyway, after he left that night, I decided then and there that the hair issue was a deal breaker for me. If I continued to see him and he did cut my hair, I could envision myself committing murder.

Did I have PMS at the time? I can't remember. It didn't matter. All I knew was that I would not put myself in a position for him to follow through. You might say, "It wasn't that serious. It's just hair." Yeah, well, fuck you, too. No one has the right to do anything to me against my wishes. You either accept me as I am or not at all. I will make changes to my appearance as I see fit, as I want to, and on my own terms. I want women to recognize controlling behavior in all forms. I want you to stop a relationship at any point in time if you are uneasy. No dick is worth losing yourself.

I called him to tell him it was over but got his voice mail. Yes, I left a message. I didn't even tell him why. I just said that I wouldn't be calling him again and for him not to call me. I like it when men respect that and don't try to keep calling you. It just pisses me off more when they try to keep calling.

Being a comedian, I jokingly told my brother, "Remember I told you I met this guy who was the male me?" He said, "Yeah." I said, "Well, it's over. I got tired of myself."

Delete Mr. Likes to Play with Scissors's number. Now I can comfortably go back to enjoying my hair. Next ...

Pictures

Please listen to me, people: do not believe that guys look like their professionally done pictures. If you personally know someone who has had headshots done, ask to see the pictures. They do not look like the person. You will be very, very disappointed. Trust me. How do I know? Can't you guess? Yes, it happened to me before … a couple of times. I'm forever optimistic, remember.

If they have additional photos posted that are regular pictures, make sure and check those out thoroughly and come on back to the real world. You can use the professional one to judge how they might clean up. You will never see them this perfect again, though. But dare to dream.

Many people post the dates of their pictures, but some do not. I say if you are not sure, go ahead and ask how old the photo is. If the guy gets indignant, tell him to kiss your ass in Macy's window. That only means he does not look like the picture. Do not take his reaction personally or second-guess your request.

If they do not have any photo at all, it is up to you to request one. My feeling on this is that he is hiding something if he hasn't posted his picture from the beginning. The few that I requested a photo from were definitely not worth it, not that good-looking. The other main reason that a guy won't post his profile is that he is a serious player and doesn't want other women catching him still on the site. He may even use two or three "no picture" profiles to play an even broader field. The player will also get sexual in writing with you very quickly, which is another clue. Once again, this might be something you're looking for. If not, just block him, and he won't be able to contact you again.

The other player is the one with the ultra sexy shots. He is trying to allure you. He knows he is fine and sexy as hell, plus he knows how to work it. If you want to play, go right ahead—he is the king of the playground. Remember, he is only for play.

When a guy posts a zillion pictures, ten with his animals, six with other people, and four of various rooms in the house, it just creeps me out. I don't know why. I look at them, and all I can think is "why?" Why do I want to see a picture of your kitchen? Cars, I get: it's the penis extension thing. If I analyze it, it may mean he is not comfortable with just himself and may think the only reason someone would want to be with him is if he has many possessions. On the other hand, he may just be a photography buff, but I tend to think too much.

If a guy has several photos and is not smiling in any of

them, take it as a sign. The sign is saying that he needs to go to the dentist. I have encountered this scenario a few times. I even asked them why they were not smiling, and the answers have been varied, but all were lies. Their teeth were jacked up: crooked, missing, discolored, and, lest we forget, gold.

Now, on some sites, the person gets to describe their looks. I have only seen two out of hundreds describe themselves as "stunning looking." They were delusional. You've got to have some really big cojones to describe yourself as stunning looking. I would like to think that they meant it as a joke, but you never know. There were several guys who described themselves as very good-looking and were not. I report this after actually having met them in person.

Now, I believe the rule of thumb for describing yourself should be that many, many people have already told you to your face that you are what you describe. In this way, you are not conceited, you are convinced! It is not what you think but what the masses have concluded. I know for a fact that one guy could not possibly, ever, have been told that he was very good-looking. There have been times when I thought someone was all right looking from his photo, but his description said good-looking, so I gave him a chance. I have been pleasantly surprised. I was not pleasantly surprised when one Mr. Very Good-Looking was more like Freddie Krueger. *Very good-looking? Very good-looking? Where? Here's a mirror. Where do you see very good-looking?* I know that's not nice, but it is, however, the truth. They say pictures are worth a thousand words. Yeah, well, not meeting someone in person is worthless.

Cheese ...

He Is Just Strange

There are many who fit this category for a wide range of reasons. One guy's screen name was Destiny Framed. He told me he printed my picture and framed it—a little spooky. There was one who said he was a preacher but that I shouldn't tell my friends. Why? Perhaps because everyone would also know he was full of shit? He was a preacher, so he didn't like for me to curse. I told the prude personally, and it was also on my profile, that I had a mouth like a sailor. Why would he keep calling me? I kept cursing, and he kept calling. Finally, he said to me, "I told you that it is offensive to me when you curse." Fuck you.

"I told you that I curse," I said. Some people are slow learners. Why did he think he could change me? *Bye-bye. The truth shall set you free.*

I met Mr. Paranoid at a Starbucks in Compton near my job. He sat down, and his head was turning from one spot to another.

"I know they're all around," he said.

"Who?" I asked, while my facial expression showed that I was scared of the impending answer.

"Thugs, guys with guns, ready to shoot. I know. I was one."

"What are you talking about?" I asked.

"I can see what you can't," he replied.

Alrighty then. He wrote me an email later that night explaining how years ago people had wrongly accused him of something, and he went to jail and lost everything. Now he was living in a special apartment complex where there were many rules and regulations—no drinking, no drugs, a curfew, lights out at midnight. Not that I needed another reason to never see him again in life—but a curfew! That was just the icing on the cake. Good luck in finding another paranoid gun mate. We don't even need to mention that you've been to prison.

If a guy starts sending you emails with extensive sexual questions, just go ahead and block him. Immediately.

If you meet someone, and he wants you to sit on his lap or close to him with legs touching within the first ten minutes, "Run, Forrest, Run!"

If he has four cats, he is the equivalent of a crazy old lady. I, personally, am allergic and could not imagine even one cat. Just say no.

Man, it is scary out there …

Been to Prison: The Saga Continues

Now, as I mentioned, I actually had "been to prison" written in my profile as a deal breaker. It is also deal breaker #3 in this book.

1. The author. We spoke on the phone several times, and he seemed all right—"seemed" being the operative word. He told me he wrote a book and had another one about to come out. I wrote the title down and looked it up on amazon.com. Then, I went to the publisher's website and found a brief bio on him. He was a troubled youth but turned himself around while incarcerated. He earned a couple of degrees. Let's mull that around a few minutes. You have to have done quite a lot of time in order to get a couple of degrees. *Hello? Goodbye. Incarcerated. What is "Don't talk to me" for $500, Alex?*

2. The cab driver/screenwriter. We talked for a couple of weeks before meeting at a Starbucks. The meet and greet went quickly because he was acting strangely. He showed me a screenplay he had written, which, he told me, was loosely based on his life. I skimmed a couple of pages, read something about a guy who had been to prison, and suggested he make me a copy so I could read the whole thing at my leisure. The way he was acting made me nervous, so I was trying to cut the meeting short. Again, I knew I wouldn't be getting the whole script to read—ever. The point was to walk away peacefully. I found out later that he had indeed been to prison. I believe that men think that since they have turned their life around, anything can be forgiven. This might be true of someone that you have some history with, maybe.

3. The cousin of a famous rapper. Of course, he, too, had a great deal of charisma. He looked very sexy in his picture, another one the camera loves. We met, and he immediately told me how much he loved my haircut. Years ago he had gone to cosmetology school and studied hair. He wasn't too much into the makeup aspect. *Hmmm. File that: low-level gay.* We talked about liquor and our likes and dislikes. He really liked cognac but also quite enjoyed white zinfandel. Hmmm. *File that: priority gay.* When he told me he had been to prison, I looked at him with wide, questioning eyes. Talking very slowly and emphasizing each word, I asked him, "You've been to prison?" He said, "Yeah, twice, actually. Just for drugs. Mostly, I had them for my cousin, but I got caught with them." I was stupefied. Been to prison twice. Hmmm.

"Did you not read in my profile that I don't date guys who have been to prison?" I asked.

"Yes, but I've turned my life around and have been straight ever since," he replied.

Normally, I wouldn't say anything outright but rather file it. However, I was just done.

"I'm really happy that you've learned your lesson and turned your life around; how-else in-ever, I wrote that for a reason," I said.

Gay and had been to prison twice. The man of my dreams, or should I say nightmares?

Get the fuck away from me.

Bye-bye. My name is Kim. Keep it movin'…

Just a note: I think that when I stated I preferred not to date guys who had been to prison it had the opposite effect. If I hadn't mentioned it I probably wouldn't have been contacted by so many who had been incarcerated. My bad.

Mr. Insensitive

I think this was my longest "internet dating" relation-ship—six weeks! Well, maybe. Actually, I was away for one of the weeks. He had a job, a car, and an apartment, and didn't stress me out. Little things mean a lot. He neglected to initially tell me that, besides an eighteen-year-old, he also had a ten-year-old. How convenient. I guess when guys see "I don't do kids" on my profile, they feel the need to hide them. They actually think that once I get to know their children, I will come to love them. They are sadly mistaken. I truly do not want to interact with little kids.

I knew this relationship was not going to go anywhere. I liked him OK, but it wasn't earth-shattering or anything, by any means. At least he was very attentive to me in the bed-room, and that was a very nice change. Let's face it, it was just sexual: a distraction, a dalliance, if you will. He didn't rock my world, but he shook the neighborhood. Plus the kid, remember? However, those things aside, it still doesn't mean

I will go ahead and accept just "anything" behavior-wise. I still need to be respected as a person.

Scenario: One Friday night he called me to ask if he could come over. I said fine. He told me he was close and that he should be at my place in about ten to fifteen minutes. He never showed up and never called. The next day, Saturday, I still didn't get a phone call. I finally called him at about five that night. I questioned him about what happened.

He replied, "What happened with what?"

I asked, "Didn't you call me last night and say you were coming over?"

He told me he did, but he explained how he had a problem with his car, called his friend to help him, and that was that. *Really?*

"What about calling me?" I asked.

Of course, he was in the middle of something, couldn't talk then, and would call me back. Whatever. He never called me back, but he stopped by on Sunday. I asked him for an apology.

"An apology for what?" he asked.

"How about common courtesy to let me know you were all right, not in an accident, etc.?" I replied.

He said, "I don't think I owe you an apology."

Really, asshole. That's what people from Earth would do: apologize. "Well, if your daughter, eighteen years old, called you and said she'd be home in fifteen minutes, and you didn't hear from her that night or the next day, you wouldn't be worried?" I asked.

He said, "No."

OK, you're a nonfeeling, insensitive, moronic asshole. What kind

of parent or person is that, just from a purely human standpoint?
"What you're saying to me is that you don't give a shit about anyone," I said.

He left, still oblivious about his actions.

Now, I am a writer, and there are many guys who have received "Dear John" letters from me in the past. Mr. Insensitive had a fax machine, so I wrote out how I felt and why and said goodbye. It has been my experience that some people don't "hear" what you're saying but can finally get it if it's in writing. If you get a letter from me, be afraid. Be very afraid. It is over.

Bye-bye. Delete Vinnie Barbarino's number.

(Character from the television show *Welcome Back, Kotter*, famous for saying, "Who?" "What?" A kind of oblivious person!)

He's Just Not

If you haven't met him yet, only talked on the phone, and he constantly calls you asking if he can come over and "kick it," block his number.

If you haven't met him yet, only talked on the phone, and he constantly interjects "isms" into the conversation so that you have no freakin' idea what he is talking about, let him go. *Where am I, in the middle of a Jeopardy show? What is "I don't give a crap what you're talking about," Alex?* This is another way he tries to make himself seem like he knows more than you. It's also another way to make himself feel superior. *Well, he can be superior all by himself. Duh! Help me, I'm stupid.*

If you have talked on the phone for a month, and several times he has told you he will call you to set up a time and place to meet but has never called, drop him like a hot potato. Mr. Elusive has problems, and you don't need to waste your time finding out what they are.

A guy I had talked to for a few weeks called and told me

he had to go into the office (which was in close proximity to where I lived) and that he would call me in a few hours so we could finally meet. How did Jamba Juice sound for a meeting? Fine with me. He never called. Not to set up a meeting, not to say he couldn't make it, and not to say fuck you. As a matter of fact, I might have felt better if he had called and said fuck you. My feeling on this is there is no need to ever call me again. If he can't even use common courtesy, why should I bother with him? Some may say I shouldn't be so tough. Hmmmm. I think they are the ones who are gluttons for punishment.

There was a guy I dated years ago who I didn't meet on the Internet. I told him I did not answer my door if anyone showed up unannounced. The first time he showed up unannounced, I figured he might not have heard me. I told him again and let it go. The second time, I figured he must have forgotten. I told him again and kept my eyes open. The third time he showed up unannounced, he got cursed out, not let inside, and told goodbye. Three strikes, baby. If you get three strikes, count yourself lucky that you lasted that long. Most never make it that far with me.

My longest relationship since being divorced but before this internet dating saga was a booty-call relationship that lasted a year and a half. Maybe I should psychoanalyze myself about this and see why that is exactly. Anywho, this guy never listened to me. I repeatedly told him that I did not eat sweets. He kept bringing me sweets. Here's some pie. Here's some cake. Here's some ice cream. *Mothafucka, can't you understand English?*

When someone consistently does not listen to you, pay

attention to that. They are definitely not into you. I was not into him "in that way," so it didn't bother me as much as it might have in a serious relationship. It just pissed me off that I had to keep repeating myself.

Let's get into booty-call relationships for a second. They can be quite useful at different times in your life. They should be stress-free; otherwise, what is the point? No going out, no dating, no sleeping over, and no cooking. I told my guy, "You need to eat before you come, and when you get here, you need to eat before you come ..." Yeah, baby!

The moral of that story is: it's OK if he's just not—as long as you're just not.

Weird First Emails

Here is an actual email I received (it has not been corrected grammatically). It covers both deal breaker #1 and #3:

I was just looking at some women who viewed my profile and seen your picture. First let me say that you are beautiful and that you have the right to decide what you are looking for in a man, but why do women put stipulation on love? How can you say that you don't want some of the things you listed? The only reason I say that is because some of that list is me and I can't change that. But one thing I can change is me, and as of today, I have, and I am very proud of myself for that. I have kids, and I take care of them. [His profile said he had six and two live with him.] I have been incarcerated and done my time, and I don't think that society has the right to continue to try and hold me back. Because of the mentality of people like yourself—no offence—you will never know that the one you turned down could have been the one for you. I just thought I would get that off my chest because I made my mistakes, and you have too, but you haven't got caught!

My response:

> I used to believe, as you do, that you can't put a stipulation on love—then I grew up! First, I can say, "no little kids" because my son is twenty-six, and I have no more patience for little kids. "Ain't been to prison" is a personal choice. I'm glad you turned your life around, and I am happy for you, but that doesn't mean I want to date you— my prerogative, as they say. "My mentality," as you put it, is that I know exactly who I am, what I want, what I don't want, and what I will accept—nothing else. I know my mistakes. They are not a secret, and if any man does not want me because of them, I understand. You need to learn not to take shit personally and get over it. If I don't know you, how can it be against you personally? My profile is all about me.

Let's stay with the "don't take it personally" scenario for a moment. What people do and say really have nothing to do with you and vice versa. When you understand that people are consumed with their own reality and aren't thinking about your needs and wants, you will be saved from needless suffering. This lesson is hard to learn and practice, but it can free your soul in the long run.

One of my sayings is "Am I bothering you?" If what I am or am not doing does not affect you one way or another, why would I care what you think? I don't have to justify myself to you. Women need to stop worrying about others' opinions and concentrate on their own.

Email #2

Hello, i am a new guy to this dating site.i am BJ.i got to see your profile while browsing and i think we could talk more.at first i thougt its mere stupidity trying to find a relationship on the internet,but when my friend actually got married to that fat angel i beleived there is more to this whole internet love affair.i am really praying hard so it will work out good for me too.i have tried 2 visible relationships around me and i realized its a mess up. i pick up interest in you while i read through your profile,but can i really count on it?am confused.could you explain to me why you needed a true relationship now on this website?have you tried others before that never work out for you too? pls i really need answers to this.i will wait for your reply soonest.......you can talk to me at XXX@yahoo.com.

Commentary: Why would I reply to that?

Email #3 (You will be as mad as I was when I finished reading this.)

Hello,

How are u doing?..i hope u doing good well i am "C" 44 male from West virgina i work as a building contractor...well it nice coming accross your profile and i think it really intresting...You want to be treated right. You want to be valued and understood. You want to be free to express yourself and you understand the world around you. You are strong and passionate, intense and gentle. You are attracted to a man--not a wisp of a man. You value depth and character, integrity and passion--not market campaigns or elevated superficiality. Do you like productivity and intensity?--I am only interested in women that have a sense of self, not a sense of what they want others to perceive them to be. Be productive not consumptive. I like action that produces positive results, not action for the sake of action. If you think you have some depth let know we are together..If you are interested in getting to know someone that is in control but not controlling, knows exactly what he wants, and is passionate and intense about life--look no further. I am very happy with who I am--I am intense and very passionate. I am also very selective. I can talk to people and look them directly in the eye. I have an artists heart, creative and seeking the asthetic--I love photography and creating or enhancing images that catch the eye--I love music and musical composition--I enjoy academics and theory, I enjoy utilizing my brain and my communication skills...What i do for fun.....i love swimming....playing football and tennis....travelling....fishing and so on...and i will like to move out like having a dinner with a lady whom both of us are honest and sincere with each other...go to beach,Cinema and play golf is she likes playing that game....I'm a passionate, sensitive and caring man who is not afraid to show his feelings. I'm a very tactile person and would like my date to be the same type of person. Touch is such a wonderful way in which to communicate. Too many people out there are afraid to share that type of communication with each other. I'm open and honest and attempt to treat everyone with respect. I'm not infallible and I do make mistakes. I would like to meet someone who can be forgiving and try to perhaps see things from the other side. Remember, I don't have to be wrong, for you to be right! I enjoy spending time with people. both inside and outside. but also need and enjoy having my alone time. I'm a romantic and enjoy spending time with a lady who is able to share herself with me physically, spiritually, and emotionally... i guess i am going to stop here..well if u would like to talk more and to make me your friend and see what happens later u can IM me to xxxxxx@yahoo.com or u can IM me to my yahoo messanger xxxx care to hear from u soon Take good care of your self

Commentary: I was exhausted when I finished reading that.

Too many issues, too little time. I wanted to kill him. Is that wrong?

If he has more issues than *Playboy*, then "he's just not!"

Email #4

I think your past with other men have led you to be too suspicious.

I am who my profile *discribes*.

It *seem* you are more into the physical part (looks, size, *ect*).

I am sure you are a good woman.

Best wishes to you in your search and Journey.

Commentary: The above was in response to my asking if his picture was current and if he had a full-body shot. I had seen his picture online for about a year, so I knew it was at least that old. You will notice that he never answered my initial inquiry—because he doesn't look like his picture! He said his build was athletic, yet he won't post a full-body picture. Hmmm. Plus, can you say "spell-check"?

The first impression is important, so please make sure and triple-check what you have written before you send it. You also want to make sure it doesn't babble on or scream "crazy." Keep the initial email very, very simple—for example: "I'm interested in conversing with you further. Write back if you feel the same." Your profile should be where more in-depth information is first seen.

Profile Spelling

This is the first introduction to the person you want to meet, date, sleep with, and maybe even marry. Pay careful attention. I'm going to show you some of the mistakes that have caught my eye and made me hit "next."

I have an easy manor (manner)
I play bid whish (whist)
I was marriage (married)
Through my hold life (whole)
I'm looking for someone who knows there passion (their)
You should know where your going (you're)
I like mistery books (mystery)
I'm stubbord (stubborn)
Weather I agree or disagree (whether)
I am so important about basketball (what?)
I'm speachless (speechless)
I'm concederate (considerate)

In my spear time (spare)

I like being intamate (intimate)

My profile discribes (describes)

Yahoo massanger (messenger)

You are very intresting (interesting)

Seeking the asthetic (aesthetic)

You're very spacial (special)

I am layed back (laid)

I was seperated (separated)

I want to larn to fly (learn—Maybe you should larn how to spell first.)

I am a gentalman (gentleman)

This forty-eight-year-old guy listed as his occupation "education." Interesting. I would really like to know in what capacity. Here is an excerpt from his profile and my corrections are in parenthesis: "I prefers to comunicate (communicate) buy (by) telephone rather than buy (by) computer. I am looking for a person who is a good comunicater (communicator). Also they should want to enjoy life despertly (desperately). Like travling (traveling) and most definetly (definitely) spending qualitiy (quality) time together."

People, please use a dictionary. Use spell-check. Ask a friend to read it first. Something. Anything. First impressions are lasting impressions. You should at least appear somewhat literate. I don't care how much education you do or do not have: there is no excuse for so many misspelled words. I had a hard time just trying to type these words incorrectly because my computer wanted to correct them.

Speaking of education, I may not have attended college, but I still got my master's degree. Thank you very much. I am not ashamed to admit it. I, personally, was homeschooled. My master's is in penisology! The tests were really, really hard. There were a lot of open-book tests. Truth be told, I did fail the course a couple of times—on purpose. Practice makes perfect. No, seriously, as it turns out, I had a learning disability. I'm dickslexic. On the plus side though, I can use either hand because I'm ambidickstrous.

Friends have asked me where I come up with some of my words. The dicktionary, of course! I'm currently working on my PhD (which stands for proficient in handling dick). We should always strive to better ourselves.

I'm sorry, did I get off track?

How to Keep from Meeting Me—
in One Phone Call

His profile read "There are five important keys to life for me, and money is not one of them. Trust, honor, respect, friendship, and love."

He emailed me first. Oh, by the way, his screen name was "blkjoystick." Hmmm. Really. Very interesting. The statistics: he was thirty-seven years old and had three children. I wrote him back, asked how old the children were and for a photo of him since there wasn't one posted. He replied that he didn't have a photo (how convenient) but that he resembled Jeffrey Osborne, the singer. His children were twenty-three, twenty, and seventeen. He gave me a telephone number. I had to call. I swear that sometimes I feel like I'm perpetually driving by the site of some train wreck and just have to stop to look.

"So, you had your first child at fourteen years old?" I asked.

He said, "What are you talking about?"

"You have your age as thirty-seven years old," I replied.

He said, "Oh, that was a mistake. It should be forty-seven."

Hmmm. First lie uncovered.

He proceeded to talk, and I just listened. Women, shut up and listen. You'll be surprised at what people will tell you. Since the age was a lie, I asked about his height. Yes, he was five-feet eight-inches. His profile said that his build was athletic. He told me he weighed one hundred ninety-eight pounds. So, he was short and fat. He told me he was at the Veteran's Administration Hospital. I asked if he worked there. No, he was a patient! He had been there for one year. Apparently, he had had several hernia operations, and they hadn't gone as planned. I'm sorry for laughing. So, he was a short, fat, dick-not-working, jobless guy. What a catch.

He told me he had a girlfriend last year. She was white and had two small kids. He met her at an AA meeting. Ummm.

I asked, "So, you're in AA?"

"Yes," he said. "My drinking and druggin' days are over."

OK, I had to cover the mouthpiece on the phone so he wouldn't be able to hear my hysterical laughter. So, he was a short, fat, dick-not-working, jobless alcoholic. *Can it get any better than this?* He continued his story about how there was too much drama with this girlfriend. She called him on New Year's Day to report a major "baby daddy" problem. He rushed over there by bus. Yeah, that's what I said—by bus. File that. He said he really liked her, but it was too much drama for him. Of course it was. He already had his own baggage. As a sidenote, he mentioned his car blew a head gasket and that he was trying to save up to get it repaired. So, he was a short, fat, dick-not-working, jobless alcoholic with no car. Copy that. Eureka! Everything I was looking for in a mate.

My girlfriends once again accused me of lying. I was starting to feel set up. These could not have been this person's real circumstances, not to mention that he was actually admitting everything and still trying to get laid. He may not have had a whole helluva lot, but he had big balls. Even if they weren't working too well. Poor lamb.

He told me he had a way to get money. I didn't even ask. He told me he was going on a journey. OK, now I couldn't resist. I asked, "It doesn't entail a spaceship, does it?"

"No," he replied. He didn't even get the sarcasm of the question. He was a little slow. He used to ride the short yellow bus. Beep-beep.

Did I mention his profile also listed him as self-employed? Well, in his defense, they didn't have a job choice of "unemployed," so self-employed was the closest choice since it had the word "employed" in it. You can't be mad. So, he was looking for his soul mate as well as a job. I inquired as to what job he had prior to being hospitalized. It turned out he was a counselor for mental patients. *Hmmm. He could be his own client.* Am I the only one who finds this whole scenario a tad funny?

On this particular day, though, and at this point in time, he would take any position. He stated that if he were to be a garbage man he would be the best garbage man that he could be. There you go: a good outlook and a great way to think in order to start over. It was up in the air, but at some point he might decide to stay in California in lieu of returning to Maryland.

He still had one problem, though, in that he had constant

pain as a result of the operations. Maybe he should start drinking again. I'm joking! Lighten up.

No way, no how was I going to talk to this lunatic any further, much less meet him. Most women are trying not to get a DWI. I'm trying not to get a DWA, "dick with aggravation!" This one was knee-deep in it. See ya, wouldn't want to be ya.

Later that day, I called my ex-husband since he loves a good laugh. I know that sounds strange; however, I have known him since I was five years old, and, although we have been divorced for five years, he is still my best friend. No one knows me better. We still communicate about our respective friends and partners or whatever you want to call them. I recapped this conversation for him. He was howling. At one point he told me to stop because he was starting to cry. I had to be making this up. He told me, "He sounds like a keeper." Then, he kept laughing.

I also remembered that the nut had told me he was used to dating white women and was now looking to try dating women of color. I asked my ex, "Do I look like a fuckin' guinea pig?" Not in this lifetime, buddy. Try hitting on someone else. Maybe someone who is deaf, dumb, and blind.

I didn't know I could actually meet someone who could encompass so many deal breakers at once. A couple of my male coworkers have jokingly told me that my standards are way too high and that I will never get what I'm looking for.

How depressing is that thought?

How to End a Relationship in Four and a Half Hours

I talked to him on the phone, and we had an instant connection. Many of my initial conversations seem to start this way, huh? He was so funny. I smiled the whole time we talked on the phone. He was only two years younger than me. Good age. I met him at yet another Starbucks. Oh my goodness, he looked way better than his picture. What a refreshing change. Yeah, baby. I had previously told him that I'd once been on a date with a pimp. So, when he came up behind me and asked, "You got my money?" I died laughing.

I got my tea and we sat down, but now he was on his cell phone. He gave me the "I'll be with you in one minute" finger. He finally finished and said, "You know, I could really use a stiff one."

In my comedic mode I was thinking I should say, "Yeah,

I could use a stiff one myself!" But I refrained and just said, "No problem."

So we went to this Mexican restaurant, another love of mine—not, and ordered a couple of drinks. As we chatted over cocktails, I began to loosen up. In no time I worked up the nerve to tell him about the white zinfandel theory. Then I asked him, "So, do you drink white zinfandel?"

He looked at me like I was crazy and said, "Hell no."

OK, he passed that test. I just wanted to see his reaction. I find this little storytelling a quaint way to ask a question without actually asking it. So anyway, we had this great chemistry. Later, when he walked me to my car, we kissed. He was a fantastic kisser. He was into me, and I was into him—big time.

I kept my wits about me, said goodbye, and drove home. He called me about twenty minutes later. He asked me if he could come over, and after trying to play a little hard-to-get, I said yes. *So much for being good.* Then I remembered that I can do what I want, when I want. Picture now the defiant little brat you used to babysit, asserting with hands on hips, "You're not the boss of me." I know myself, and if I want to sleep with someone, it's because I want to, and I will not beat myself up, no matter what happens down the road. I'd like to add that it's called "being grown-up." Actually, it's called "acting like a man."

Go Kimi! Go Kimi! Go Kimi!

I gave him the address. He arrived, and I was immediately glad I let him come over. We were still very comfortable and continued chatting, and I put some music on. He was feeling a little warm and took his shirt off. Wow! The body—oh my God. The body. He was so fuckin' sexy. Did I mention the body? You women know how we can get—anticipation. Damn—oh my God. Did I mention the body? If there was any trepidation before, it was now out the window. We took a shower—separately—and then it was on.

Oh my God, did I mention the body? I don't think I ever had sex so many times in one night. It was a very, very long night indeed. He used his four condoms, and thank goodness I had more. Whoa. Damn. (When I told my girlfriend, Michelle, this part, she politely called me a slut puppy. I politely told her, "Judge not, lest ye be judged.") I am forty-seven years old, and while I can't "drop it like it's hot," I can lean it like it's warm! Did I mention the body? I think I did. However, I didn't mention the unseen parts. My, oh, my. I hit pay dirt, baby. Needless to say, we didn't get much sleep.

I remembered that I had some frozen homemade dinners left over from Thanksgiving, so I heated one up for him to eat for breakfast. He needed a big meal—trust me. Yes, I can cook, and he was very grateful for the chow. Then he had to go and pick up his truck for a run to Florida. Yeah, I know—after this great night of passion or lust or whatever, he had to leave for two whole weeks, damn it all to hell. He left, but, needless to say, I was a very happy camper at work that day. I'm sorry; I lost my train of thought. Did I mention the body?

OK. So, I know what you're thinking: I was sprung. Well, maybe in one respect. I *was* head over heels in lust and giddy as hell—I admit it. Now, as I said, he was going to be away for two weeks. It seemed like an eternity. We talked about five times a day. He was so sweet. I would call, and he would answer the phone, "Hey, my love," or "Hi, love of my life," or "Hey, sexy," or "How's my baby?" or "Hey, gorgeous." I could go on and on. (Michelle said, "Please don't.") It made me feel really special and the center of attention.

Of course, he was on the road, so I had a captive audience. He was driving about four hundred miles a day. He told me how he was tired of dealing with young girls and wanted a real woman. Well, he lucked out on that one. This was a whirlwind romance via the telephone. At least it gave us a chance to get to know each other better and take a breather, if you will.

Oh, I forgot: I got a call from another guy about two days after I slept with "the trucker." I answered my phone, and he said, "Hi, it's George." I didn't know who the hell I was talking to. He said, "You don't remember me?"

I said, "No."

He said, "Damn, you hooked up with someone who put it down so good you forgot who I was?"

I said, "Honey, he put it down so good I forgot my own name."

Anywho, the trucker and I sent e-cards back and forth, and soon there were just two days left until he'd be back to me. That was the longest two weeks. Yeah, don't celebrate too soon ... he called and said such and such happened, so he would be detained another two days. I was so dejected. Bummer. Truth be told, I was also thinking, "Great. Now he will be back just in time for my period!" (Michelle: "Thanks for sharing." *Oh, grow up.*) He was originally due back on Tuesday. Now, he'd be back on Thursday.

But guess what? He surprised me and called me Tuesday

night and said he would be in at midnight. Yeah, yeah, baby. When I heard his deep truck horn, "beeeep beeeep," I ran to the window. I was in my house yelling, "It's him, it's him!" like the scene from the movie *Overboard*. (Michelle read this and said she was going to throw up.) I put on some sneakers and ran across the street to the truck, climbed into the cab, and kissed him hungrily. It was yet another scene from a movie, and I felt ecstatic and silly. It was nice to know I could still feel that way.

We went back inside my apartment, and we were cool for a while, just happy to finally be back in each other's company. Eventually, he went to take a shower, and then I fed him some real food, as opposed to the fast food he'd been eating on the road. Cut to yet another memorable few hours in the sack. Wooo! Remember the line from that Jeffrey Osborne song, "Can you Woo Woo Woo?" Damn! Let me tell you, it was a woo woo woo extravaganza. Did I mention the body? Needless to say, I was late to work that morning. Who knew? The trucker now had to complete his run to Bakersfield. He would be back on Friday. As I figured, I got my period on Thursday. (Michelle: "TMI.") No problem, since this was just the beginning of our relationship; we would have plenty of future time together. Little did I know …

I was off from work from that Thursday, December 22, until the end of the year. I also have a gift basket business on the side (haveyoulostyourmind.com), so I was still busy filling those orders, which, fortunately, kept me occupied. I did buy the trucker a couple of little things for Christmas, which was that coming Sunday. He had also told me he had a seven-year-old son. I know, kids are one of my deal breakers … but did I mention the body? Plus, he said he and the mother did not get along well, so I just figured the child would be with the mother. So anyway, while shopping, I picked up some videos and toys for him to give to his son. I knew that since he was on the road, he didn't have any time to shop. Yes, I do try to think of other people's predicaments and, if I can, help them. Plus, it makes me feel good, too. (Another girlfriend: "Or you're just a sucker.")

On Friday he called to let me know he would be over at about 4:00 PM. His trucking partner was picking him up, and he asked me if it was OK for his friend to just drop him off at my house. Seemingly, this would ensure no time would be wasted and that he would be by me that much faster. Sure, no problem.

Four and a half hours and counting, starting from 4:00 PM. He came inside, and he was hyper as hell, in a good way. He told me his partner just presented him with a great deal in which he would only have to drive locally and work three to four days a week. He was pumped. This was a great opportunity. He wouldn't be away from me for two weeks at a time. He showed me a list of brokers and asked if he could use my computer to start doing some groundwork. I said sure and told him I would be right back. I had to go around the corner to the store for some shipping paper and would be gone about ten minutes.

Let the implosion begin …

He called me five minutes later on my cell phone to tell me that he invited his partner over for dinner. Yes, you read that right. He invited someone over to my house for dinner without asking me first. Next, he told me, "I saw you had some shrimp in the freezer," (I had put vodka in there for him, so he had seen the shrimp) "so can you make shrimp, linguini, and white sauce?"

This mothafucka has lost his damn mind, is what I thought. "No, and I'll be right back," is what I said. You know that I was trying to remain calm, cool, and collected en route to my house.

When I got home, he was still on the computer. I went to fix a drink, eggnog with cognac, and lit a cigarette. From here on, when I say eggnog, feel free to assume that cognac was also added, not sparingly. I went over to him and said, "You know, you really should have talked to me before inviting someone over to dinner."

He was fuckin' oblivious. He said, "Why, what's wrong?"

I said, "I have been working all day, I'm tired, and now I also have to clean off the kitchen table." I didn't even get into "how about common fuckin' courtesy" and "it's not your damn house."

His response was "It's OK. He's cool. He can eat anywhere." *File that.*

When I told my girlfriends this story, they all asked, "Did you kick his ass out right then and there?"

"Nope," I said. "I obviously needed more incentive." I also knew I had PMS and how we women can be during this time, so I was trying not to overreact. I tried to tell myself it was me, not him.

I had some steaks marinating in the fridge for us, and there was enough for three people anyway. While I was cleaning off the kitchen table, he went into the kitchen and tasted my drink. "Wow, this is good. Can you make me one?"

Are your fuckin' hands broken? is what I thought. But I held that in and fixed him some eggnog. Anyone who knows me well would be able to read my face immediately. Like I said before, he was oblivious. This is one way to tell when people don't care about your feelings, the situation, or pretty much anything that doesn't pertain to them. They see nothing.

Mr. Hyper started a new conversation in the kitchen. "Yeah, so I'll only have to work three days a week and make as much as if I were working seven days. Don't hate me, but you'll be getting up and going to work, and I'll still be in bed sleeping."

You would be in whose fuckin' bed sleeping? is what I thought. I just looked at him incredulously.

Then he said, "I have a big-screen television in storage. We can put it in the living room and then put your television in the bedroom."

I said, "I don't watch TV in the bedroom."

He said, "Well, I do." Is it me, or is his ass trying to move in? Oh, and don't think for a minute I didn't catch the fact that he said his TV was in storage. *Why is it in storage? File that.*

He stepped outside to my little yard area and said, "This is a great spot to barbeque. We can get a grill. I am an excellent barbeque-er."

"We" who can get a grill? I asked myself. *"We?" This is strictly a "me" residence. I'm getting a headache.*

He went back to the computer and got on his cell phone. I made another eggnog and lit another cigarette. While holding out his cell phone, he called to me and said, "This is a coworker, and she makes gift baskets, too. Talk to her."

I looked at him and adamantly mouthed, "I don't want to talk to her."

Again, Mr. Oblivious Trucker said, "No, she's cool. Talk to her." I wanted to punch him in his fuckin' face. I took the phone, politely had as brief a conversation with this stranger as I could, and handed the phone back to him. He was all happy, and my glaring look still didn't register. I needed some more eggnog. Deep breath. Deep breath. Did I mention the body?

Back on the cell phone, he was now talking to (I could tell from the conversation) his baby's momma. I left the kitchen and stepped outside to my little yard. He finally came to me and said, "I was talking to my son, and there's something wrong. He gave me the code words that he needs to be picked up right away." Wow. Now, remember, his partner dropped him off, so his car (which, at this point, I was doubting even was his car) wasn't at my house. He asked to borrow my SUV to pick up his son, who was only ten minutes away. I immediately felt concern for the child, of course, so I said sure. I had been having car problems, so I told him to also let me know how my vehicle was acting.

After he left, it hit me: *Shit, he's bringing his kid back to my house!* I fixed another eggnog and called my ex-husband. Ronnie answered the phone, and I said, "You are not going to fuckin' believe what is going on." I had already told him about the trucker, but I brought him up to speed. He laughed hysterically, mostly because he knew how I felt about kids. Can you say "Cruella DeVil"? I kept yelling, "Oh my God, he's bringing the kid here. He's bringing the kid here." I heard more laughter from Ronnie while I was fuckin' freaking out.

He told me to calm down and said, "You know what you need to do." I heard a knock on the door and hung up the phone. *Here we go, here we go, here we go …*

I opened the door, and there was the trucker with his son and an armful of clothes. Yes, an armful—not a change, but a backpack and what looked like enough clothes for a week—in his arms. I needed another eggnog. Fast. The kid was nice, well mannered, and cute. But I don't like kids. Yes, I know I have a son, but he is now grown. I went and got one of those videos I had bought, told him it was an early Christmas present, and turned it on. I beat a hasty retreat to my yard with my eggnog and cigarettes. *What the hell have I gotten myself into? I was trying not to go ballistic. Is the yard spinning?*

In all of the drama, I forgot his friend was supposed to be coming for dinner. Damn. I told him to call his friend, but there was no answer. "Look," I told him, "I am hungry, so I'm fixing dinner." *Oh fuck.* I remembered that I now had to cook for the kid too. *Where the hell is the candid camera? I know I'm on that mothafucka.*

Cut to dinner. I cooked the kid's meat well-done and cut it up. *Didn't I finish doing this shit fifteen years ago?* I must confess again that the child was really nice and well mannered. That, however, does not mean I liked him. I was indifferent. I couldn't care less. Bite me, that's who I am, and I will not make any excuses. Mr. Oblivious Trucker said something to the effect of "This is nice, but Kim is looking kind of iffy."

I looked iffy? Did I look iffy meaning uncomfortable, put out, and imposed on? *Kiss my ass, and fuck you.* We finished eating, and I cleaned up. He came in the kitchen to ask if I needed help as I finished cleaning the last freakin' utensil. How gallant. You and I know how men plan that shit.

His son was back in my living room watching the video, so I went back outside. Yes, I had my eggnog. The trucker joined me. He was once again on his cell phone with his partner, standing opposite me and smoking a cigar. I listened intently to his conversation about his child's mother. It went a little something like this: "Yeah, man, I was talking to her, and she put my son on. He was talking to me and then gave me our code word for something being wrong. You know, she's just been out of rehab for a couple of months, and she seemed like she was drinking again."

I was thinking that he was the one who drove her to drink. I'd been moving in that direction ever since his partner had dropped him off a couple of hours ago.

He continued, "When I got there, I could smell gas escaping. The stove was on, and she didn't smell anything. If my son hadn't given me the code, he might have been dead in the morning. Yeah, man, I'm gonna get a two-bedroom apartment," (*File that*, I noted) "and take my son and keep him full-time. I'm gonna get a nanny, and I won't have to even deal with her."

I think fast, so I could envision him having a nanny problem and asking me if I could babysit. Forget the spinning feeling: it was earthquake time. I needed another eggnog.

Then he told his friend, "Yeah, and I got the perfect woman." I looked him dead in his face, serious as hell, and shook my head no. There was not a glint of a smile on my face. I could tell that it finally registered with him that something was amiss.

Once he hung up, he said, "Why did you shake your head no when I said I had a good woman?"

I said, "No, you said a perfect woman, and I am not perfect. I'm feeling quite a bit overwhelmed right now. I've also been working hard all day, my back hurts, and I'm tired."

Mr. Oblivious said, "Why don't you go in your room, lie down, and relax?"

"Because I don't want to go to my room. My entertainment area is in the living room. Maybe I would like to watch a movie—and not a kid's movie," I explained. He looked off into space.

I asked him if he could take his son to his sister's house. He actually said, "He is not her responsibility." *He ain't my fuckin' responsibility, either*, is what I thought.

He told me he was glad I said something then and didn't wait until morning. *Wait until morning? You mothafuckas would have been dead.* Remembering the TV-in-storage confession, I asked him if he lived with his sister. He never really answered that directly but did fess up that he had given up his apartment a couple of months ago and was mostly living in the large cab of his truck. *Bingo was his name-o.* Like I said, I knew he was trying to move his ass in. Sorry, but the dick was not outweighing all the other shit. He might have been able to play that game with me when I was twenty years old, but at forty-seven ... not a chance. I don't need any man that bad.

Next he said, "Maybe I should call a cab and take my son to a motel."

I threw him for a loop big-time when I said, "OK, I'll get the phonebook." I got the number and told him I would call the cab for him. Thankfully, the cab was there in fifteen minutes. I helped him with getting all his son's stuff out to the cab. I gave him a kiss on the cheek and said, "Take care." He called me about an hour later and asked if I was relaxing, and I assured him that I was. The last time I spoke to him was the next day. He called me, and my answers were extremely short and monotone. I was done. Finished. Finito.

Delete Mr. Trucker-Trying-to-Move-In's telephone number.

No letter. Not even a Post-it.

Four and a half hours. Is that a world's record of some sort?

FYI: I have since quit smoking. Truth be told, I am glad I did not try until after this experience. I am sure I would have relapsed.

How to Start and Stop a Relationship in Three Days

After having dealt with men my own age or younger, I was ready to give someone older a chance. He had to be more seasoned, I reasoned to myself. Checking in at fifty-six years old, this gentleman was the oldest one I had ever talked to or emailed. Maturity had to have settled in by now. That, at least, might be a plus.

We spoke everyday, sometimes twice a day, for two months. He told me that he was a very serious person but did like to laugh. Hmmm. As we all know, once it's out that someone is a comedian, the jokes start popping up. He tried. On the phone he tried. *File that.*

He lived about one and a half hours away from me by plane. He was also about twenty minutes from my cousin's house, so I wasn't too ambivalent about making the trip. Plus, he had a very secure government job and was about to retire.

Therefore, this was a person who didn't want to do anything to jeopardize his future, if you know what I mean.

I called him as soon as the plane landed, but he still kept me waiting for a half hour. *File that, too.* OK, I realize that he had a cable television repairman at his house; but he left him there to pick me up, so he could have also left him there to pick me up on time. I'm just sayin'.

He looked OK. Like he had told me, he wasn't a "pretty" man, but he wasn't horrific by any means. He was not as tall as I prefer, yet still OK. I called my girlfriend once I was in the car with him, and she told me to put him on the phone. He told her that he was quite happy, did not take anything not offered, and had no desire to go to jail. He gave me the phone back, and I assured her I would check in often. I had already given her all of his information: name, address, and telephone numbers.

He drove me on a brief sightseeing tour of some of the properties he was inspecting. The conversation was light and comfortable. We headed to his house because, as I said, he had left the cable repairman there. The house was gorgeous. It was a bi-level house in the hills of northern California. He showed me to the guest room, turned on the big-screen TV, and went back upstairs to deal with the repairman. It was now about four in the afternoon. He checked in with me often, apologizing for this work taking so long. Around five o'clock, he made us these microwavable spaghetti and meatball bowls. He added some extra cheese to them to spruce them up, and that was fine—something to hold us over until dinner.

I showered, changed, and was ready to go out by about seven o'clock. We went to this hotel that had live jazz adjacent to the restaurant and bar. We ordered drinks, and he said hello to a couple of people he knew. I picked up the menu whereupon he asked, "Are you hungry?"

Uh, yeah, ya' think?. "Yes, I could eat a little something," I said. I don't even remember what I ordered, but I know he got the ribs. How could I ever forget the sucking and smacking sounds? He cleaned those ribs, let me tell you. This scene reminded me of the bottomless pit guy. He damn near ate a loaf of bread, too. Have you ever had the pleasure of watching someone eat as though it was his or her last meal? It's special.

Shortly thereafter, he excused himself to go to the restroom. He was gone forever. I thought he fell in. When he finally returned, he gave me a key chain—a silver high-heeled shoe. OK, that was sweet. We returned to his place, messed around a little, and then went to sleep.

The next day the cable repairman had to come back because something still wasn't working correctly. I was once again watching the downstairs television and thinking about food. Here he comes to save the day: I got another spaghetti and meatball bowl, yes, with extra cheese excuse me, for brunch. More spaghetti. Readers, please feel free to use this as a guideline on how not to feed or treat a houseguest.

That night we went out to a karaoke club. Thank God they served food. After we finished eating, we went to the other side of the club to watch the karaoke and relax. I enjoyed listening to the singers, but I could have done without the teeth-sucking sound effects to remove food from his teeth. It was quite annoying, and I was ready to punch him in his fuckin' face, too. Sorry, I have an issue with that particular habit. My stepfather, whom I loathed, used to do the same thing. Shoot me. I see faces being smashed when I hear that sound. I think that's a normal reaction, don't you?

When the karaoke was over, a DJ came on, and the place turned into a dance club. It was very cool. We danced and danced, and I ended up having a great time.

On the way home, he stopped at the supermarket to pick up a few things. I was guessing he needed more spaghetti and meatball bowls. Can you feel the sarcasm?

When we got back to his place, he lit a fire. We had some more drinks, chatted, and played the touchy-feely game. Things got hot and heavy. In the middle of all of this, he asked me, "Is it everything you hoped for?"

Huh? If by "everything" you mean a big stomach, a small dick, insufficient foreplay, and a "wham bam thank you ma'am" session, yes, my expectations were more than met. "Ummhmm," is what I said.

The next day, Saturday, it was raining and cold. He took me to brunch. I actually escaped a spaghetti bowl—wow! I had this great seafood quiche, and he went all out: bacon cheeseburger and fries. The diet plate. He had to keep that stomach stretched. You know, it hit me that he had told me over the phone that his body looked so much better than men ten years younger. I guess that would be true if you were hanging out at Overeaters Anonymous.

In the quiet of the restaurant, the chewing, smacking sounds while eating with his mouth open couldn't be masked. I kept looking out of the window. After the meal, he stopped in the men's room. Once again, he was gone for quite a while. After a few minutes, I decided to go to the ladies room. I stood in line, handled my business, and was still done way before him.

Everything literally went downhill from here …

We went sightseeing. The first stop was San Quentin. Yep, the infamous prison. Don't ask me, I have no fuckin' idea either. We sat in the car looking at the prison. I wish you could have seen the expression on my face. Besides that, I was speechless. He pointed out where the death row inmates were housed. A picture would have more than sufficed.

Next stop was the Golden Gate Bridge. Remember I told you it was raining? You can't really see much through all of the fog. We got out of the car, and he opened the umbrella only to have it flip backwards from the wind. That happened twice more before I grabbed one end of the material to help hold the umbrella down in front of us like a shield. I was scared the wind would catch the umbrella and send us airborne off the damn hill. When we reached the top, he saw that I was pulling on the umbrella material. Next thing I knew, he snapped at me, "Don't break it." *Break it? Fuck the umbrella. What about me?* In a snippy way, I said, "The wind broke it when it flipped it backward four times." *You materialistic son of a bitch.* While he was trying to resuscitate the oh-so-fragile umbrella, I pretended to be interested in a plaque with information about the bridge on it. Like I gave a shit. I was wet and cold.

He said, "Maybe this wasn't such a good idea." *Ya' think?* We headed back to the car. He took off, walking six feet in front of me. I plodded along behind him in utter amazement. I told myself to closely study him to see if he would ever turn around to check if I was OK, had slipped and fallen, had hit my head and was bleeding to death. Nothing. Nada. Zip. Zero. Zilch. He did not look back once. *Son of a bitch. File that. There's a reason why some people have never gotten married.* When I got in the car, through the door he didn't open for me, he asked if I had a tissue so he could wipe off his glasses. *Yeah, you'll find that dry tissue in the same place as your fuckin' brains.* "No, I don't," I said.

Next, he took me by some places that he said he would have taken me if it weren't raining. I thought, *Where am I, in sightseeing hell?* We drove past Chinatown. We drove past Ghirardelli. We drove past the tallest building—the name of which I honestly don't remember. I had obviously given up paying attention anymore. *Is he actually driving my ass past shit I'm not going to stop and see?* "Hmmm ... Wow," I said.

We got back to his place about five o'clock. He had gotten tickets to see comedian Mike Epps later that night. I went to take a nap, exhausted mostly from aggravation. He woke me up at seven. We had to leave by eight, even though the show was at ten. The club was in San Francisco, and he correctly predicted the parking would be horrendous. We ended up driving around and around and around. He complained the whole time, even though he knew it was going to be that way. Then I realized that some people just get off on complaining. He was getting on my nerves, again.

Hey, a parking space. Thank you, God. I needed to laugh so bad after this long, disastrous, wet, windy, no-sightseeing day. San Francisco is known for its hills. Well, we were three long blocks away, and two of those blocks were hills. It had stopped raining, but the streets were still wet. I took the umbrella that I had packed just in case. Let the downhill games begin.

He took off walking again, as he had earlier, and was now about four feet in front of me. I looked at the back of his head in total amazement. I was taking baby steps, trying to make sure I didn't lose my footing and then slide all the way down the two blocks. He gave less than a fuck, obviously. Wait a minute, wait a minute. He was slowing down.

Forever optimistic, I thought he'd finally realized his lack of manners or human qualities and would now wait for and assist me. Instead he turned to me and said, "You go on ahead; I'll be right there." I continued walking but stole a backward glance as he—can you guess? He went between two parked cars and PEED! Stop laughing. Stop saying, "Oh, hell no, he didn't." I never in my lifetime thought I would need to add to my deal breaker list "does not pee in the street." Just when I thought you could take some things for granted. Back to life, back to reality… Remember in the movie *A League of Their Own* when Tom Hanks yells at a female ball player, "There's no crying in baseball"? Well, *yell with me everyone*: "there's no peeing in the street on a date."

At this point in relaying this story to my girlfriends, they said, "What the hell did you do?" I said, "Well, actually in the moment I told myself to file it and concentrate on not falling down. I would process the fact later that he needed some Depends."

Mr. Pee Pee Man caught up to me and, yes, passed me straight away. As he breezed past me I couldn't help but be relieved by his ungentlemanlike conduct. At least I wouldn't have to deal with pee pee hands. When he got to the corner and started crossing the street, I yelled out, "No, it's OK. Go on and cross the street without me." If he heard me, he didn't react and kept going. He only stopped once he got to the line for the show.

That was fucking amazing. I had never been treated like that in my life by anybody. *Someone is getting ready to tell me I've been punked, right? Come on, stop playin'.* I arrived and didn't say a word. He picked up right where he left off, complaining. Now, because it took so long to find a parking space, we were stuck far back in the line. He said, "I will never come back here again." Sarcastically I responded, "Neither will I. Ever." He didn't get it. This was the most obtuse mothafucka I have ever met. Complaining, complaining, complaining.

At one point, he said, "I wonder if I can get a refund."

I said, "Why don't you go and find out?" He just looked at me. I just looked at him. My look was not a nice look. I heard someone yelling at the line, asking if anyone had tickets to sell. I said, "Yeah, right here," and pointed to Pee Pee Man.

He had the gall to look at me like I had lost my mind. "What did you say that for?" he asked me.

"I don't know. Maybe because that was what you said you wanted to do—sell the tickets," I replied. This is really funny.

He said, "What's wrong with you?" Finally, he showed a flicker of recognition that I was pissed off (excuse the pun). When I mentioned his not helping me down the hills, his response was, "You didn't ask for help." What that response showed me was, besides not being a gentleman, he had no common courtesy at all. I mentioned something about his being serious, and his biting remark—directed toward me personally was, "Well, I don't laugh at *everything*," which was supposed to be a jab at my lightheartedness, continuous laughter, and ebullient personality.

Once again, fuck you. I said, "I have never laughed so little in my entire life." He stared at me, and I stared back at him. *Are we having fun yet?*

The line started moving. He said, "How about when we leave I go get the car while you wait here?"

I said, "Thank you. That would be very nice."

We got inside and were shown to our table, and when I turned around, he was not there. I assumed he went to wash his pee pee hands. Or maybe it was time to pee again? Whatever. By this point I was beyond caring about his bladder issues. I was determined to enjoy the comedy show. He returned, and the waitress came over. I ordered a drink and some food.

He looked at me questioningly and asked, "You're hungry?"

"Yes. I haven't eaten since brunch, ten hours ago."

Then, he asked, "Didn't I feed you some chicken strips this afternoon?"

No, Mr. Selfish, thinking only of your damn self. You probably fixed yourself something to eat while I took a nap. "No, you didn't," I said.

Would you believe he ordered more food for himself, too? The show started, and I was screaming and laughing as loud as I could. Make a smartass comment about me laughing, will you. He would rue the day he ever made that remark, let me tell you!

I had an absolutely fabulous time: a) because he didn't say anything; b) because he didn't say anything; and c) because he didn't say anything.

So, I had found the key to enjoying time with Mr. Pee Pee Man. I needed to live in a comedy show, and he needed to be a mute, close to a bathroom. Utopia. How sad a commentary is that? Of course, all good things must come to an end. Alas, there was still the ride back to his place. He went and got the car as he previously promised he would. It was the one gentlemanly thing he had done, and I had to bitch to even get that. We arrived after a long, long, long, awkward, silent ride. Once inside, I think he was trying to make amends for being an ass. I know why. All men know why. Because they want sex!

And the Oscar goes to ...

He fixed me a drink. I turned on the TV. He asked me if I was still pissed.

Pissed? Am I still pissed, you dense ass? "Oh, please. I let that go a long time ago. I'm fine. Please!" I said. Then I gave the dismissive hand wave. Throw up time: "I had a great time. The show was absolutely hysterical. Thank you so much." We chatted for a while longer.

It was very late, about three in the morning, so he said, "Go get changed, and come up to bed."

"I'll be right there," I replied. I went to the guest room and changed into my negligee. Yes, I can hear everyone screaming at me, "What the hell is wrong with you?" Well, let me finish, will you? I went upstairs and got into bed. I told him I had a bad sinus headache, had just taken a couple of pills, and needed to wait for them to kick in. Sure enough, he fell asleep. Whew! Eventually, I too dozed off.

I don't know how long afterward I was awakened by some chewing, smacking sounds. Here we go again. He had fixed something for himself and only himself. *Un-fuckin'-believable*. When he finally finished scarfing down his chicken tenders, I could smell them, he drifted off into a deep, snoring coma. Oh my God. It was sooo loud. I quietly got up and went back to the guest room where I had peace and quiet. The silence was truly welcome.

The next morning, I could hear him in the kitchen, but I wasn't ready to get up yet. Plus, I figured if I lay low, so to speak, there would be less time to interact. I needed to be at the airport by two thirty. I went back to sleep and eventually emerged, showered, changed, and packed, by one o'clock. I was starving. I went into the kitchen and made some tea. There were some Cheez-Its on the counter, so I started eating them and turned on the TV.

When he finally came back downstairs, he was carrying his Tupperware with the remnants of knockwurst and a piece of baked potato. "Good afternoon," he said.

"Good afternoon," I replied.

"The snoring ran you off last night, huh?" he asked.

"Ummhmm," I answered.

He noticed me eating the Cheez-Its. "Hungry?"

"I sure am." I could taste the knockwurst and potatoes, baby.

Would you believe he fixed me a fuckin' spaghetti and meatball microwave bowl, again? *Get me out of this spaghetti hell.* "Thanks so much," I said.

All I could think about was how the next hour was going to be one of the longest in my life. Finally, time to go to the airport. I made the most inane conversation along the way. I spotted the airport sign, hallelujah. I could see the terminal. Ten, nine, eight, seven ... I got out of the car and took a deep breath of air. He took my bag out of the trunk. I could taste my escape. I gave him a kiss on the cheek and said, "Thanks again. I'll call you to let you know I got in OK." He drove off.

I entered the terminal, went through security, and headed straight for the bar. I ordered a glass of wine and told the waitress to keep a running tab. I planned on knocking 'em back very quickly.

Before I boarded the plane, I went in search of some real food to eat during the flight. If I so much as heard spaghetti mentioned, I might have hurt somebody. Fortunately I found some baked chicken, homemade mashed potatoes, and veggies. I hope no one on the plane saw me eating this food. The food was actually more orgasmic than he was.

I was ecstatic to be back in my own house. That little adventure felt like doing time in prison, including the freakin' prison food. I called Mr. Pee Pee Man and told him I got in OK. That was the last time I talked to him. I sent him an email the next day. The email was nice, but to the point and clearly not open-ended. I did not mention any of what I just wrote. I just said that he was a very serious person and that I was not.

Delete Number ...

Having to add "does not pee in the street" to my deal breaker list: priceless.

Recap: I need to explain some of the decisions I made during the end of this trip. After the peeing in the street, making my way down the street solo, and then his nonstop bitching, I took an inventory of the situation. I was in San Francisco, far from his home and far from where my stuff was. It was already late, and I didn't want to impose on my family. It was a whole bunch of stupid shit, nothing really major, and nothing I couldn't handle. "Buck up, take a deep breath, and get through it," I told myself.

So, I made the best of the show and made sure I enjoyed it. Later, back at his place, I decided to do the acting "over it" scenario because you never know how people will react when confronted. Think of it in terms of backing a dog into a corner. I had no desire to test him, especially being out of my element. The lesson here, ladies, is that we must always think before reacting. Don't cut off your nose to spite your face.

Many, many of my friends gave me advice on what I should have done or how I should have reacted. I'm sure some of you reading this have received similar "suggestions" from your friends. Never second-guess yourself. Do what you feel is right for you in the moment and to keep yourself safe. "Woofing"—going off on someone—should be put on the back burner until you are safely surrounded by a crowd of people.

You do not have to be nasty. Know your circumstances. Do not antagonize in a car or where there is no clear way out. Be cool and agreeable until you are safe from any potential harm. Think smart. In general, and this is just me, I try very hard not to be intentionally mean to anyone. No matter what, it's more important to be nice.

BOB: my battery-operated boyfriend is looking really good right now!

Deal Breaker List

I asked some of my friends for their deal breakers and to share some of their answers below. Please feel free to add your own!

Hygiene

- Bad breath
- Dirty nails/nails that are longer than yours/one long nail
- Stinky feet
- Nose hair/picks nose
- Ear hair/dirty ears
- Yellow teeth/doesn't floss/missing teeth
- Gold or anything other than enamel teeth
- Braided beard

- Long hair on back/body
- Waxes
- Pimply/pockmarked skin or face
- Smack on back and pimples pop
- Body odor/bathes in cologne
- Member has more bumps than a French tickler
- Uncircumcised
- Skid marks on undershorts

Manners

- Chews with mouth open
- Talks with food in mouth
- Licks fingers (not at KFC)
- Picks teeth at table
- Sucks teeth (trying to dislodge food)
- Doesn't open doors
- Doesn't help with bags
- Walks on inside of sidewalk
- Walks ahead of you
- Ignores you when walking on precarious sidewalks, etc.
- Not in vocabulary: thank you, excuse me, God bless you, I'm sorry, please

- Burps loudly/does not cover mouth

Questionable Sexuality

- Wears poom poom shorts (Richard Simmons)

- Your friends, especially your gay friends, tell you their "gaydar" is going off and ask you, "Are you sure he's straight?"

- Has had a gay experience (once a switch-hitter, always a switch-hitter)

- Wants to attend gay pride events with you

- Has track lighting

- Drinks white zinfandel

- Knows more about fashion than you/wants to share your clothes

- Tells you he was "tickled pink" that you called

- Wants to decorate your house (This may be OK!)

- Looks at nails with hands outstretched and palms down

- Looks at bottom of shoes over the shoulder

In the Bedroom

- Does not eat kitty

- Your vibrator is bigger

- Premature ejaculation

Body Jewelry

- Nose ring
- Eyebrow ring
- Tongue ring
- Nipple ring
- More piercings than you

General

- More than one baby mama
- Unemployed/on general relief/out on disability
- Has roommate (especially mom)/you can't or don't go to his house
- No car
- No bank account (or strictly cash dealings)
- No computer and/or illiterate
- Works at your job—a no-no
- Been married more times than Elizabeth Taylor
- Wants you for a green card
- No personality
- Wants to move in after three dates
- Only gives you a cell phone number, no work/home number
- Married/tan line on left ring finger

- Comb-over

- Hair is in cornrows (braids)

- Weighs more than your car

- He says he loves you within one week (or he asks if you love him within one week)

- He acts clingy (excessive "Where are you?" and "What are you doing?")

- He wears the crotch of his pants at his knees

- Christian/church employee and wants to sleep with you on the first date

- Has been on the game show *Cheaters*

- Has been sued on *Judge Mathis* (or any judge show) for not repaying a loan

- Just strange

- Drinks too much/smokes cigarettes or cigars

- Does drugs

- Likes to play the "what if" game

In the end you need to ask yourself: deal or no deal?

My Deal Breakers

Fill in the deal breakers that apply to your own preferences.

1) _____

2) _____

3) _____

4) _____

5) _____

6) _____

7) _____

8) _____

9) _____

10) _____

Kim Samuels

11) _____

12) _____

13) _____

14) _____

15) _____

If you have many more, you might want to seek therapy!

The Telephone Dilemma

Time and time again I hear women and men trying to figure out exactly when to call members of the opposite sex. You just met, there is a mutual attraction, and you tell each other you would like to get to know one another better. How often should you talk? Are there any rules, spoken or unspoken? I asked a few people who I thought should or might know.

Q: If the other person called the last time, is it now your turn?

A: Grow up! There are no turns.

Q: What is the appropriate length of time between telephone calls?

A: Forty-eight hours max

Q: How many messages can you leave before not making another call?

A: Two general messages (not clingy)

The general consensus is that if you feel like calling someone, do it. Do not count "days." My personal position is that I put myself out there if that is how I am feeling. If you don't go all out in each and every relationship, you are not giving each one the energy that it deserves. Later on you might start questioning yourself: if I had done such and such, maybe the outcome would have been different ... By not holding back, you will always know and be satisfied with how you handled yourself. Then you can tell yourself, "It's not me: it's him! You can also say, "I was great, he was an ass, and he lost the best person he will ever meet."

Yes, there are rules!

1) If you initiated the call, and you don't get a call back within forty-eight hours, you are being played.

2) If the other person initiates the call to you, and you don't call back within forty-eight hours, you are a player and you know it: clap your hands!

3) You should call back ONLY if he or she leaves a general nonclingy message. Example of a general nonclingy message: "Hey, what's good? Give me a call when you get a chance." Example of a clingy message: "Hey this is _____. I called you, but you didn't call me back. I hope everything is OK. Are you all right? Here's my number just in case you lost it or something: Home is ____. Work is ____. Cell is ___. My ma's house is___. Call me anywhere, anytime."

** If you leave this kind of message, get help. You have issues and need to step away from dating.

FYI: A real player waits for no one. It's his or her world!

By the way, telephone calls to new acquaintances should never be made after nine o'clock at night or before nine o'clock in the morning on weekdays. I say no one should ever call anyone early, before noon, on Saturday or Sunday. That is just not respectful of people who like to sleep late or just need to have some quiet downtime. Do not even dare trying to give the excuse of wanting to make some plans on those days. Plans for the weekend should be made no later than Wednesday prior to said weekend. What about being spontaneous, you say? Fine, I understand that, but it should also be understood that it might be misconstrued as, "What, does he think I don't have a life?" Save the spontaneity for when you know someone a little better.

Ladies, remember the time when there weren't any cell phones or voice mail, and you would just sit at home waiting for the phone to ring? You could always use the excuse that he might have called but you weren't at home. Nowadays, there is no excuse for someone not to reach you if they really want to. You better buck up and not take it personally if a guy doesn't call you back. If he is not interested, let it go, because it is not about you. It's about him. The sooner you realize this, the sooner you will stop spending time feeling bad for absolutely no reason at all.

The Pre-Stalker

I talked to him on the phone after exchanging a few inconsequential emails. I told him that we might be able to meet up upon my return from a weeklong business trip. I mentioned to him that my flight was leaving at 8:00 AM the next day. My cell phone rang at 6:00 AM. First, I don't do mornings. Second, remember the time restrictions on calling someone you don't know? I did not answer the phone. He left a message to have a safe trip. Thank you, that was nice. Early, but nice.

He called me at 12:30 AM that same "night." That is three and a half hours past the 9:00 PM cutoff time. *I don't know you, and do you own a damn watch?* Where does he you get off calling me at these inappropriate times? Two strikes.

Day three: I got an email that read "thinking of you." Noted.

Day four: call but no message.

Day five: call but no message.

Day six: my return home date. Call with a message to have a safe trip back. So, now we are at five calls and not one return call. Let's recap from the previous chapter. If you don't get a return call after two messages, you do not call again!

Day seven: two calls and one message.

Day eight: call and the message "This is your new husband." *My new what?*

Day nine: call at 7:00 AM and a message that maybe we could get together for lunch or dinner. In case you missed it let me reiterate: he called me at 7:00 AM Yeah, readers, I know you feel me on that one. *Leave me alone and get a life.*

Next, I gave Mr. Gas Station Man my business card with my cell phone number on the back. This encounter was on a Saturday afternoon. My phone rang at nine on Sunday morning. Do you need to ask if I answered the phone? I didn't think so. He called next on Monday morning at seven o'clock. Great, I've met yet another person who's an early bird. I answered the phone, but I was "nicety." That means that I was nice while at the same time nasty. I explained how I was trying to get ready for work, that it was very early, and that I would talk to him later.

He called me later, and we spoke briefly. He told me he had a gift for my house. He told me he had a gift for my house. I know I repeated that sentence. I wanted to make sure you got it right. I asked myself, "Why?" He proceeded to tell me that he had a gift certificate for (he starts sounding it out) "May. May. Make." He asks me to help him out. I was thinking about gift certificates and where it could possibly be from, and I came up with Macy's. Yes, I was right, and now I knew that besides being unable to tell time, he was also illiterate. There would definitely not be a date.

If you dare try to make me feel guilty for that decision, smack yourself. He also called my job and my cellphone from numbers I would not recognize, trying to fool me into answering. Sorry, hip to that game, too. After many, many unreturned calls I was forced to call him and leave a message that someone I was seeing off and on was back on again. I told him he should discard my number—then I remembered he may not know what that means—or throw it away.

My friend La Tonya and I call all pre-stalkers by the same name: "Jo-Jo." This is a reference to the movie *Jo-Jo Dancer, Your Life is Calling*. Only it's more like "Jo-Jo the stalker is calling!" We'll call each other and say, "Would you believe Jo-Jo called me again!" The real name doesn't even matter, and we get the connection immediately.

Follow the rule: if you call twice with no return message, do not call again. It will save you precious time that might be better used elsewhere. I know for whom the bell tolls, and it is not you.

My Profile:
As Posted on a Real Dating Site

I was on several throughout the year—predominantly African American dating sites.

A little about me:

Drama free, and I intend to keep it that way! Life is too short for BS, and my radar detector is extremely accurate. Only those who keep it real need apply. I don't have time for game playing, and honesty is the best policy. I laugh a lot and am ebullient (not silly). I can dress up or down, and I am at ease in either attire. Self-confidence—no problem here! I am very spiritual: a true believer, but not fanatical.

What are you looking for in a partner?

Looking for someone who is honest—tell me why this is so hard!

Deal breakers: Have little kids, been to prison, live with yo' mama, gold fronts, and definitely dicky-doo. That's when yo' stomach sticks out further than yo' dicky-doo! Hey, I work hard at staying in shape, and I want someone who feels and does the same. I am a firm believer in "when people show you who they are, believe them." Treat people how you would like to be treated. Not looking for and don't need a one-night stand—if you are, keep it movin' ...

I'd just like to add:

I love to swim, enjoy walking by the beach, and work out five days a week. Love seafood, sushi, and most foods—not much into Mexican. Like old-school R&B and some new stuff. Can dance but mostly do so in my living room. Am adventurous but need someone to be adventurous with. I don't mean camping, sorry!

I can have a mouth like a sailor, so if that bothers you, then don't bother with me... I am grown and will not be changing anytime soon. Straight up, now tell me...

On a Serious Note:
He's Just Not to the Tenth Power

I know I have joked a great deal about some of the deal breakers that I have encountered along the way. However, I need to be very serious about some things, too. Women have to take active responsibility for watching out for signs of mental and physical abuse. I have heard people say that there weren't any signs. No, you either did not see them or chose to ignore them. On this point, I do not have any jokes. I was sexually abused from the time I was twelve until I was thirteen years old. My stepfather physically beat me from the time I was nine until I was thirteen years old. I was mentally abused from the time I was eighteen until I was twenty-five years old. I am obviously speaking from previous experience.

Of course, as a child the signs were not mine to see or ignore. As an adult, however, I can tell you that if a man ever raises a hand to me—much less hits me—it is over. No second chance. No explanation required, expected, or accepted. This goes for any time in the relationship, starting from day one.

Physical abuse is easy to see and feel; mental abuse can be a little trickier. It can be something as small as criticizing you about something you do or as large as removing you from contact with friends and family. It's called controlling.

Controlling behavior tends to start out with simply making you feel slightly uncomfortable. You tell yourself that he loves you and would never do anything to intentionally hurt you. You let it slide. Eventually you find you have to let everything slide until you have given up control and are just a puppet. You move like a robot. You are detached and numb. How do I know? Because I lived it, sister. I was so deep in the trap, my mother thought I was totally brainwashed and was acting like a zombie.

Would someone who really loves you make you feel like that? I don't think so. Anyone who is not supportive of you, your goals, or your dreams does not belong in your life. Period. FYI: this pertains to friends as well as family. If you are seeing someone who is rude to others, be very leery. If he is disrespectful toward strangers, chances are he will be disrespectful toward you. Do yourself a favor and walk away before you get too involved.

My friends say I don't give guys a chance. I say guys are the ones who blow their own chance. I only pay attention. Why should I waste my precious time with someone who does not even meet my lowest standards? Do you women hear me? If I set the bar so low that an ant can get over it and a guy can't, why should I feel bad for saying adios?

You may ask me why I even set the bar low. I'll tell you why. This will knock so many people out of the ring so quickly, it will make your head spin! We waste time by setting the bar high. How so? In waiting to see if the person will reach it, we miss the fact that their ass should have been gone a long time ago. I know it may sound weird to set the bar low, but really think about it. This is such a time saver. You might tell a friend, "Oh, he's not that bad." First of all, any sentence with the word "bad" in it is not good! If you say that, smack yourself.

> You say: "He's not that bad. He only hits me when dinner is late."
> You should say: "That son-of-a-bitch hit me! And he actually thinks he's going to get away with it."

> You say: "He called me stupid. He just had a hard day at work and didn't mean it. I know he really loves me."
> You should say: "I am stupid ... for being with him! Fuck him. I deserve much better than that."

> You say: "He never calls me to let me know if plans have changed or when he's going to be late. I'm used to it now."
> You should say: "I won't accept not being acknowledged as important, not even one time."

One time—that's just me. If you want to, you can invoke the three strikes rule here. If you let this continue further, I can guarantee you that you will end up regretting it. You will end up waiting for one reason or another for the rest of your life.

Stop making excuses.

You say: "You know, he didn't do such and such because blah blah blah." I say: "You know, he didn't do such and such because he's an asshole." Period. Bottom line. There is no need to sugarcoat shit. It is not about you. Someone else's actions have nothing to do with you.

There is no need to feel bad when relaying a story about a guy who's "just not" and why you didn't stick around for more. It in no way means there is something wrong with you or that you are not worthy. He is not worthy. He can't crawl over the damn bar on the fuckin' floor! You should be proud to say "He's just not"; wear it like a badge of honor that we got it. You can say, "Yeah, that's right, I'm good," and hold your head up high. Stop accepting excuses. When someone does not respect you, he will keep coming up with excuses why he forgot you in one way or another. "I lost track of time." "I didn't have my watch on." "Was that today?" "I was tired and pulled over and took a nap." One explanation is in the title from that other book, *He's Just Not That Into You* (authors Greg Behrendt and Liz Tuccillo). I do agree that he's just not that into you, but I think that is putting it mildly and is way too dismissive of some very serious underlying issues and problems.

One extremely important life lesson that it took me eons to get: If things keep going wrong, stop. Stop. Do not continue to try whatever it is you were attempting to do. The universe is trying to tell you that you are on the wrong path or that you shouldn't be doing it. Think of it as being inside a pinball machine. You go one way and you get knocked back so you try again. You hit another blockade, so you try to reach the same goal, this time maybe through the back door. Bam!—you are turned back for the third time. Let it go. When my efforts are thwarted for a third time, I will not try again. The only explanation I need to give anyone or myself is simply "something is not right."

Practice listening to your inner voice, spirit, and intuition. This has served me extremely well. The only time things went wrong was when I refused to listen. Remember, "He's just not" is the new phrase. Whether it's that he is not worth your time, effort, or energy, no explanation is needed. When your girlfriend asks why you did not even start a relationship with so and so, just look at her and say,

"Girl, He's Just Not ..."

hesjustnot.com

Printed in the United States
115375LV00001B/114/A

9 781587 367359